I0505567

MŒRIS
And the Illustrated
Dictionary of the Ligature Œ

- WHICH Are the Words that Are Written With the
Ligature *Œ?*
- *Mœris* ASKED

Jorge A. Rodríguez
(Jar)

Text and Illustrations

Text and illustrations: Jorge A. Rodríguez (JAR)
First Edition 2007 Second Edition 2015
All rights reserved, Copyright © 2015 Jorge A. Rodríguez (JAR)
Translation: Froila Gómez
ISBN-13: 978-1511556668
ISBN-10: 1511556668
E-mail: jarrodriguezve@gmail.com
Facebook: Jorge A. Rodriguez Jar
Twitter: @jar_rodriguez

My best wishes *vœux*
to all of those
who from the heart *cœur*
read this work *œuvre*
and
also to those who
only give it
a glance *un coup d'œil*

JAR

-*Mæris! Mæris!* ...You should learn to write your name correctly... *Mæris* was already on school vacation; he was unoccupied *désœuvré* and felt his heart *cœur* in the middle of the affliction *crève-cœur*. His mother, was very sick, she had an uneasiness of which anything was known...

That morning he woke up very early and he prepared to have breakfast with his father. He had already taken out of the egg container *œufrier*, the eggs *œufs* that they would prepare for breakfast. *Mæris* ate bread, an egg *œuf* (in form of heart *cœur*) and ox meat *bœuf*; while his father also ate bread, some scrambled eggs *œufs brouillés* and salad with some poppy oil *œillette*. Both prepared to go to the clinic to visit *Mæris'* mother. In those days everything seemed to be going bad. *Mæris* in the school, always got his attention called, because, he often forgot that his name - *Mæris* -, should be written with the ligature *æ*. As *Mæris'* father had

Mœris Mœris Mœris Mœris Mœris Mœris Mœris
Mœris Mœris Mœris Mœris Mœris Mœris Mœris
Mœris Mœris Mœris Mœris Mœris Mœris Mœris
Mœris Mœris Mœris Mœris Mœris Mœris Mœris
Mœris Mœris Mœris Mœris Mœris Mœris Mœris
Mœris Mœris Mœris Mœris Mœris Mœris Mœris
Mœris Mœris Mœris Mœris Mœris Mœris Mœris
Mœris Mœris Mœris Mœris Mœris Mœris Mœris
Mœris Mœris Mœris Mœris Mœris Mœris Mœris
Mœris Mœris Mœris Mœris Mœris Mœris Mœris
Mœris Mœris Mœris Mœris Mœris Mœris Mœris
Mœris Mœris Mœris Mœris Mœris Mœris Mœris
Mœris Mœris Mœris Mœris Mœris Mœris Mœris
Mœris Mœris Mœris Mœris Mœris Mœris Mœris
Mœris Mœris Mœris Mœris Mœris Mœris Mœris
Mœris Mœris Mœris Mœris Mœris Mœris Mœris
Mœris Mœris Mœris Mœris Mœris Mœris Mœris
Mœris Mœris Mœris Mœris Mœris Mœris Mœris

emphasized it to the teachers, the moment he registered him in the school. Anyway, *Mæris* had always had the doubt, of using or not, that letter in particular that he didn't find, not even in the alphabet. He knew some words that were written with that same letter; the ligature *æ*: egg *œuf*, knot *nœud*, ox *bœuf*, heart *cœur*, eye *œil*, esophagus *œsophage*… but in occasions, those same words were written with the "o" and the "e" separate…That confused and uneasy him a lot.

This uneasiness of *Mæris*, caused that he began to notice the words more and to notice that there were others that were written with that letter, his interest for this letter was natural, after all, it was on his own name…

- *Mæris!* - His father called Him -: bring me the *œillère*, please!

- What is that? … - *Mæris* asked.

- It is the small glass that is in the other bathroom, the one that is good for cleaning the eye *œil* - the father said.

œ œ œ œ œ œ œ œ œ œ œ œ œ œ œ

œ œ œ œ œ œ œ œ œ œ œ œ œ œ œ

œ œ œ œ œ œ œ œ œ œ œ œ œ œ œ

œ œ œ œ œ œ œ œ œ œ œ œ œ œ œ

œ œ œ œ œ œ œ œ œ œ œ œ œ œ œ

œ œ œ œ œ œ œ œ œ œ œ œ œ œ œ

œ œ œ œ œ œ œ œ œ œ œ œ œ œ œ

œ œ œ œ œ œ œ œ œ œ œ œ œ œ œ

œ œ œ œ œ œ œ œ œ œ œ œ œ œ œ

œ œ œ œ œ œ œ œ œ œ œ œ œ œ œ

œ œ œ œ œ œ œ œ œ œ œ œ œ œ œ

œ œ œ œ œ œ œ œ œ œ œ œ œ œ œ

œ œ œ œ œ œ œ œ œ œ œ œ œ œ œ

œ œ œ œ œ œ œ œ œ œ œ œ œ œ œ

- *Œillère*, I thought that you would put on the eye cover *œillère (cache-œil)*, the one from my pirate costume, dad. It is that it sounds identically... why? - *Mœris* asked.

- Yes, they are words that sound and write identically; also the eye cover *œillères* of the horses are called the same... A word can, simply, correspond to different objects..., but do you see my eye *œil?* Take a look *un coup d'œil...* something bothers me in it - the father said.

- I don't see anything strange; although, it's a little red and swollen - *Mœris* told his father that continued washing his eye *œil* with the little glass *œillère*. Both left the house, heading for the clinic to visit his mother *Mœris'* father bought some carnations *œillets* to given them to his wife. *Mœris* took the carnations *œillets* and they went heading to the clinic...

œ œ œ œ œ œ œ œ œ œ œ œ œ
œ œ œ œ œ œ œ œ œ œ œ œ œ
œ œ œ œ œ œ œ œ œ œ œ œ œ
œ œ œ œ œ œ œ œ œ œ œ œ œ
œ œ œ œ œ Œil œ œ œ œ
œ œ œ œ œ œ œ œ œ œ œ œ œ
œ œ œ œ œ œ œ œ œ œ œ œ œ
œ œ œ œ œ œ œ œ œ œ œ œ œ
œ œ œ œ œ œ œ œ œ œ œ œ œ
œ œ œ œ œ œ œ œ œ œ œ œ œ
œ œ œ œ œ œ œ œ œ œ œ œ œ
œ œ œ œ œ œ œ œ œ œ œ œ œ
œ œ œ œ œ œ œ œ œ œ œ œ œ

Already in the clinic, *Mæris* sees his mother very sick, pale and thin , with a very sad and tired look *œillade*, somewhat uncombed with a careless ripple on the temple *accroche-cœur*, of those that his mother, intentionally, made with a hair dryer *fœhn* (French of Switzerland). A ripple on the temple *accroche-cœur* that took out a little smile from *Mæris*, when he saw it… he found it amusing; but soon, his little smile faded and a tear came out his eye *œil*.

- What's wrong with you, mom? - *Mæris* asked.

- I don't know, nobody knows, not even the doctors, they still wait for the results - the mother said.

Mæris' father was talking with the doctors and other relatives that were there too, as well as, an aunt of *Mæris* that was a nun *bonne-sœur* that accompanied his mother in the clinic, he uneasy and concerned listened to the doctors speak…

Mœris Mœris Mœris Mœris Mœris Mœris Mœris
Mœris Mœris Mœris Mœris Mœris Mœris Mœris
Mœris Mœris Mœris Mœris Mœris Mœris Mœris
Mœris Mœris Mœris Mœris Mœris Mœris Mœris
Mœris Mœris Mœris Mœris Mœris Mœris Mœris
Mœris Mœris Mœris Mœris Mœris Mœris Mœris
Mœris Mœris Mœris Mœris Mœris Mœris Mœris
Mœris Mœris Mœris Mœris Mœris Mœris Mœris
Mœris Mœris Mœris Mœris Mœris Mœris Mœris
Mœris Mœris Mœris Mœris Mœris Mœris Mœris
Mœris Mœris Mœris Mœris Mœris Mœris Mœris
Mœris Mœris Mœris Mœris Mœris Mœris Mœris
Mœris Mœris Mœris Mœris Mœris Mœris Mœris
Mœris Mœris Mœris Mœris Mœris Mœris Mœris
Mœris Mœris Mœris Mœris Mœris Mœris Mœris
Mœris Mœris Mœris Mœris Mœris Mœris Mœris
Mœris Mœris Mœris Mœris Mœris Mœris Mœris
Mœris Mœris Mœris Mœris Mœris Mœris Mœris

- What are x-rays? - *Mœris* asked to one of the doctors.

- They are some images, like pictures; but of the interior of the body - a young doctor that was there answered him.

- And why do they call it x-rays, doesn't it have any name?

- That is its name: x-rays; although they are also known as ray's *rœntgen*, as its inventor's name: *Wilhelm Conrad Rœntgen* - the young doctor said.

- Is it the only way to see the interior of the body? - *Mœris* asked.

- Well… - thinking a little - No, not only that way, you can also use a coelioscopic *cœlioscopie* that is a medical instrument that allows to see the body internally and this way we can take a look *un coup d'œil*. Well…, I should leave... - the young doctor said.

- Doctor. In what area do you work? - *Mœris* asked.

- I work in the laboratory, in Stoichiometry *Stœchiométrie* - the young doctor answered.

cœlioscopie cœlioscopie cœlioscopie cœlioscopie
cœlioscopie cœlioscopie cœlioscopie cœlioscopie
cœlioscopie cœlioscopie cœlioscopie cœlioscopie
cœlioscopie cœlioscopie cœlioscopie cœlioscopie
cœlioscopie cœlioscopie cœlioscopie cœlioscopie
cœlioscopie cœlioscopie cœlioscopie cœlioscopie
cœlioscopie cœlioscopie cœlioscopie cœlioscopie
cœlioscopie cœlioscopie cœlioscopie cœlioscopie
cœlioscopie cœlioscopie cœlioscopie cœlioscopie
cœlioscopie cœlioscopie cœlioscopie cœlioscopie
cœlioscopie cœlioscopie cœlioscopie cœlioscopie
cœlioscopie cœlioscopie cœlioscopie cœlioscopie
cœlioscopie cœlioscopie cœlioscopie cœlioscopie
cœlioscopie cœlioscopie cœlioscopie cœlioscopie
cœlioscopie cœlioscopie cœlioscopie cœlioscopie
cœlioscopie cœlioscopie cœlioscopie cœlioscopie
cœlioscopie cœlioscopie cœlioscopie cœlioscopie
cœlioscopie cœlioscopie cœlioscopie cœlioscopie

- We should wait and verify the results of the laboratory - the doctors said - but you should take care of that eye *œil*, you could have an infection or an ocular edema *œdème*, in the worst of the cases.

- Dad… What is an edema *œdème*? - *Mœris* asked.

- It is an accumulation of liquids that produces a swell - this way one of the doctors answered to *Mœris*, while they retired…

- Dad… What is wrong with my mom, what did the doctors say? - *Mœris* asked to his father.

- Son… they don't know it yet- answered the father that felt his heart *cœur*, in the middle of the affliction *crève-cœur*.

- You should have faith in the sacred heart *sacre cœur*, we should make vote's *vœux* of faith for your mother's recovery - the aunt of *Mœris* said, and who was a nun *bonne-sœur* and sister-in-law *belle-sœur* of *Mœris*' father.

sacré cœur sacré cœur sacré cœur sacré cœur
sacré cœur sacré cœur sacré cœur sacré cœur
sacré cœur sacré cœur sacré cœur sacré cœur
sacré cœur sacré cœur sacré cœur sacré cœur
sacré cœur sacré cœur sacré cœur sacré cœur
sacré cœur sacré cœur sacré cœur sacré cœur
sacré cœur sacré cœur sacré cœur sacré cœur
sacré cœur sacré cœur sacré cœur sacré cœur

CŒUR

sacré cœur sacré cœur sacré cœur sacré cœur
sacré cœur sacré cœur sacré cœur sacré cœur
sacré cœur sacré cœur sacré cœur sacré cœur
sacré cœur sacré cœur sacré cœur sacré cœur
sacré cœur sacré cœur sacré cœur sacré cœur
sacré cœur sacré cœur sacré cœur sacré cœur
sacré cœur sacré cœur sacré cœur sacré cœur

Mœris, remembered a friend who was an altar boy *enfant-de-chœur* and went to see him at the Church of the Sacred Heart, *Sacré Cœur*. After telling him the situation and how bad his mother was, his friend told him:

- Well… look, if the doctors don't know what's wrong with your mother, well… you investigate it. Well… I should join the choir *chœur*… - the altar boy *enfant-de-chœur* told him, retiring hastily, maneuvering *manœuvrant* among the seats of the church, and incorporating to the choir *chœur*, on the back site, the back choir *arrière-chœur* of the church.

Mœris lowered his face; he had a sad look *œillade* and, remembering his aunt's words, the nun *bonne-sœur*, thought:

- I will have faith, sacred heart *sacré-cœur*, guide me. In the back, was heard the choir *chœur* of the church intone, repeated times, ecumenical *œcuméniques* songs.

sacré cœur   sacré cœur   sacré cœur   sacré cœur
chœur, chœur   chœur   chœur   chœur   chœur   chœur
sacré cœur   sacré cœur   sacré cœur   sacré cœur
chœur, chœur   chœur   chœur   chœur   chœur   chœur
sacré cœur   sacré cœur   sacré cœur   sacré cœur
chœur, chœur   chœur   chœur   chœur   chœur   chœur
sacré cœur   sacré cœur   sacré cœur   sacré cœur
chœur, chœur   chœur   chœur   chœur   chœur   chœur
sacré cœur   sacré cœur   sacré cœur   sacré cœur
chœur, chœur   chœur   chœur   chœur   chœur   chœur
sacré cœur   sacré cœur   sacré cœur   sacré cœur
chœur, chœur   chœur   chœur   chœur   chœur   chœur
sacré cœur   sacré cœur   sacré cœur   sacré cœur
chœur, chœur   chœur   chœur   chœur   chœur   chœur
sacré cœur   sacré cœur   sacré cœur   sacré cœur
chœur, chœur   chœur   chœur   chœur   chœur   chœur
sacré cœur   sacré cœur   sacré cœur   sacré cœur
chœur, chœur   chœur   chœur   chœur   chœur   chœur
sacré cœur   sacré cœur   sacré cœur   sacré cœur
chœur, chœur   chœur   chœur   chœur   chœur   chœur
sacré cœur   sacré cœur   sacré cœur   sacré cœur
chœur, chœur   chœur   chœur   chœur   chœur   chœur
sacré cœur   sacré cœur   sacré cœur   sacré cœur
chœur, chœur   chœur   chœur   chœur   chœur   chœur
sacré cœur   sacré cœur   sacré cœur   sacré cœur
chœur, chœur   chœur   chœur   chœur   chœur   chœur
sacré cœur   sacré cœur   sacré cœur   sacré cœur

The following day before leaving the house, *Mæris'* father tells him:

- Take a look *un coup d'œil* to your shoe, take the cord, pass it by the eyelet *œillet* and make a strong knot *nœud*.

- Very well - *Mæris* answered.

- Son… there is something that you should know, your mother is not only sick, but rather she is also pregnant. You will have a little sister *sœurette*, of course, she is still very small. That is good news; although, it also complicates a little more the things …-explain the father.

- How will my little sister *sœurette* be called? - *Mæris* asked.

- Ah, that we don't know it yet, we'll see - the father answered.

Mœris Mœris Mœris Mœris Mœris Mœris Mœris
sœurette sœurette sœurette sœurette sœurette
Mœris Mœris Mœris Mœris Mœris Mœris Mœris
sœurette sœurette sœurette sœurette sœurette
Mœris Mœris Mœris Mœris Mœris Mœris Mœris
sœurette sœurette sœurette sœurette sœurette
Mœris Mœris Mœris Mœris Mœris Mœris Mœris
sœurette sœurette sœurette sœurette sœurette
Mœris Mœris Mœris Mœris Mœris Mœris Mœris
sœurette sœurette sœurette sœurette sœurette
Mœris Mœris Mœris Mœris Mœris Mœris Mœris
sœurette sœurette sœurette sœurette sœurette
Mœris Mœris Mœris Mœris Mœris Mœris Mœris
sœurette sœurette sœurette sœurette sœurette
Mœris Mœris Mœris Mœris Mœris Mœris Mœris
sœurette sœurette sœurette sœurette sœurette
Mœris Mœris Mœris Mœris Mœris Mœris Mœris
sœurette sœurette sœurette sœurette sœurette
Mœris Mœris Mœris Mœris Mœris Mœris Mœris
sœurette sœurette sœurette sœurette sœurette
Mœris Mœris Mœris Mœris Mœris Mœris Mœris
sœurette sœurette sœurette sœurette sœurette
Mœris Mœris Mœris Mœris Mœris Mœris Mœris
sœurette sœurette sœurette sœurette sœurette
Mœris Mœris Mœris Mœris Mœris Mœris Mœris
sœurette sœurette sœurette sœurette sœurette
Mœris Mœris Mœris Mœris Mœris Mœris Mœris
sœurette sœurette sœurette sœurette sœurette
Mœris Mœris Mœris Mœris Mœris Mœris Mœris
sœurette sœurette sœurette sœurette sœurette
Mœris Mœris Mœris Mœris Mœris Mœris Mœris
sœurette sœurette sœurette sœurette sœurette
Mœris Mœris Mœris Mœris Mœris Mœris Mœris

Mœris already had another reason to continue ahead with his own investigation… he wanted to discover his mother's illness and also to help his little sister *sœurette*, but… where to begin? How to discover that illness his mother has? In that moment somebody is at the door, *Mœris'* father sees who is it through the viewer *œilleton*… of the magic eye *œil de bœuf* of the door. It is the family doctor that has arrived to speak with *Mœris'* father …

- Good morning… - the family doctor greets and begins to talk with the *Mœris'* father -. I come from the clinic and not with many news, we know that she has a small inadequacy of the heart *cœur* and the stomach uneasiness continues. We believe that it is not a breathing problem; she doesn't have anything in the esophagus *œsophage* and neither a lung edema *œdème*. The estrogens *œstrogènes* she was taking were already suspended, because we don't want them to affect the fetus *fœtus*, all the corresponding electroencephalograms *électrœncéphalogrammes*

œil œsophage fœtus cœur cœur fœtus œsophage œil
sœurette sœurette sœurette sœurette sœurette
œil œsophage fœtus cœur cœur fœtus œsophage œil
sœurette sœurette sœurette sœurette sœurette
œil œsophage fœtus cœur cœur fœtus œsophage œil
sœurette sœurette sœurette sœurette sœurette
œil œsophage fœtus cœur cœur fœtus œsophage œil
sœurette sœurette sœurette sœurette sœurette
œil œsophage fœtus cœur cœur fœtus œsophage œil
sœurette sœurette sœurette sœurette sœurette
œil œsophage fœtus cœur cœur fœtus œsophage œil
sœurette sœurette sœurette sœurette sœurette
œil œsophage fœtus cœur cœur fœtus œsophage œil
sœurette sœurette sœurette sœurette sœurette
œil œsophage fœtus cœur cœur fœtus œsophage œil
sœurette sœurette sœurette sœurette sœurette
œil œsophage fœtus cœur cœur fœtus œsophage œil
sœurette sœurette sœurette sœurette sœurette
œil œsophage fœtus cœur cœur fœtus œsophage œil
sœurette sœurette sœurette sœurette sœurette
œil œsophage fœtus cœur cœur fœtus œsophage œil
sœurette sœurette sœurette sœurette sœurette
œil œsophage fœtus cœur cœur fœtus œsophage œil
sœurette sœurette sœurette sœurette sœurette
œil œsophage fœtus cœur cœur fœtus œsophage œil
sœurette sœurette sœurette sœurette sœurette
œil œsophage fœtus cœur cœur fœtus œsophage œil
sœurette sœurette sœurette sœurette sœurette
œil œsophage fœtus cœur cœur fœtus œsophage œil
sœurette sœurette sœurette sœurette sœurette
œil œsophage fœtus cœur cœur fœtus œsophage œil
sœurette sœurette sœurette sœurette sœurette
œil œsophage fœtus cœur cœur fœtus œsophage œil

were carried out and we are waiting for more results from the laboratory - the family doctor said.

*M*æris had listened sincerely and all those medical terms confused him, but soon he began to realize that those words had something in common, something that he could not still recognize fully. *Mæris* began to write some words in a small notebook in order to begin his investigation.

He went to the city library that day and arrived very tired at dusk…

- I investigated about the heart *cœur*, esophagus *œsophage* and the edemas *œdèmes*. I found a lot of information on the edemas *œdèmes* and *myxœdèmes*: brain, lung, ocular and even of the skin. The *œstradiol*, *œstriol* and *œstrone* are estrogens *œstrógenes*, these are feminine hormones. A little complicated, but on the other hand I will continue taking notes and investigating - *Mæris* thought, while he underlined words on his notebook.

Mœris, could not stop feeling some rancor *rancœur*, when believing that was his new little sister *sœurette*, the one harming his mother; but soon he would remove that idea from his head and he would put hands at work *mains à l'œuvre* to continue his investigation.

- *Mœris*, Tomorrow come with me to work, I want you to see something, we should get up very early –*Mœris'* father told him …

M*œris'* father   was the owner of a store specialized in wines *œnothèque*, he was assisting the clients the whole day with his partner *consœur*. There some objects were also sold used by the enologist *œnologues* (specialists in wine), measurement instruments, enómeters *œnométres*: to calculate the enometries *œnométries* (the grades of alcohol in wine) and all the necessary for those who love the enology *œnologie*, science of wine conservation. *Mœris* was seeing all the objects in his father's specialized wine *œnothèque* store…

Mœris Mœris Mœris Mœris Mœris Mœris. Mœris
œnologie œnologie œnologie œnologie
Mœris Mœris Mœris Mœris Mœris Mœris. Mœris
œnologie œnologie œnologie œnologie
Mœris Mœris Mœris Mœris Mœris Mœris. Mœris
œnologie œnologie œnologie œnologie
Mœris Mœris Mœris Mœris Mœris Mœris. Mœris
œnologie œnologie œnologie œnologie
Mœris Mœris Mœris Mœris Mœris Mœris. Mœris
œnologie œnologie œnologie œnologie
Mœris Mœris Mœris Mœris Mœris Mœris. Mœris
œnologie œnologie œnologie œnologie
Mœris Mœris Mœris Mœris Mœris Mœris. Mœris
œnologie œnologie œnologie œnologie
Mœris Mœris Mœris Mœris Mœris Mœris. Mœris
œnologie œnologie œnologie œnologie
Mœris Mœris Mœris Mœris Mœris Mœris. Mœris
œnologie œnologie œnologie œnologie
Mœris Mœris Mœris Mœris Mœris Mœris. Mœris
œnologie œnologie œnologie œnologie
Mœris Mœris Mœris Mœris Mœris Mœris. Mœris
œnologie œnologie œnologie œnologie
Mœris Mœris Mœris Mœris Mœris Mœris. Mœris
œnologie œnologie œnologie œnologie
Mœris Mœris Mœris Mœris Mœris Mœris. Mœris
œnologie œnologie œnologie œnologie
Mœris Mœris Mœris Mœris Mœris Mœris. Mœris
œnologie œnologie œnologie œnologie
Mœris Mœris Mœris Mœris Mœris Mœris. Mœris
œnologie œnologie œnologie œnologie
Mœris Mœris Mœris Mœris Mœris Mœris. Mœris
œnologie œnologie œnologie œnologie
Mœris Mœris Mœris Mœris Mœris Mœris Mœris

- The names of these measurement instruments are something strange… I say, they are also written with this letter, the same one that my name has - *Mæris* told his father.

- Your name is written with the ligature *æ*, like many other words –*Mæris'* father said -, in fact we gave you that name because it is written with that same letter which the name of my profession is written: The enology *œnologie*, remember that I am an enologist *œnologue* who loves his profession. Also, - *Mæris* - is the name of a king from the old Egypt and also a lake –*Mæris'* father explained.

To *Mæris* that seemed fascinating, besides that he already had written on his notebook other words that up to now he noticed that they were written with that same letter that his name had: The ligature *æ*.

- Which are the words that are written with the ligature *æ*? - *Mæris* asked.

Mœris Mœris Mœris Mœris Mœris Mœris Mœris
Mœris Mœris Mœris Mœris Mœris Mœris Mœris
Mœris Mœris Mœris Mœris Mœris Mœris Mœris
Mœris Mœris Mœris Mœris Mœris Mœris Mœris
Mœris Mœris Mœris Mœris Mœris Mœris Mœris
Mœris Mœris Mœris Mœris Mœris Mœris Mœris
Mœris Mœris Mœris Mœris Mœris Mœris Mœris
Mœris Mœris Mœris Mœris Mœris Mœris Mœris
Mœris Mœris Mœris Mœris Mœris Mœris Mœris
Mœris Mœris Mœris Mœris Mœris Mœris Mœris
Mœris Mœris Mœris Mœris Mœris Mœris Mœris
Mœris Mœris Mœris Mœris Mœris Mœris Mœris
Mœris Mœris Mœris Mœris Mœris Mœris Mœris
Mœris Mœris Mœris Mœris Mœris Mœris Mœris
Mœris Mœris Mœris Mœris Mœris Mœris Mœris
Mœris Mœris Mœris Mœris Mœris Mœris Mœris
Mœris Mœris Mœris Mœris Mœris Mœris Mœris
Mœris Mœris Mœris Mœris Mœris Mœris Mœris

- Well…, there are some very common words that for sure you have already seen: eye *œil*, fetus *fœtus*, knot *nœud*, heart *cœur*, ox *bœuf*, enology *œnologie*, egg *œuf*, esophagus *œsophage*, edema *œdème*, estrogens *œstrogènes*, sister *sœur*, choir *chœur*, altar boy *enfant-of-chœur* and others more that now I don't remember - the father answered.

- Carnations! *Œillets!* It is also written with that letter - *Mœris* said happily.

Mœris began to write all those words on his notebook, because he was realizing that there were many words in which that letter was: His father's profession, his name, organs of the body, illnesses, objects, remedies…, etc. perhaps the illness that his mother suffers is written with that letter and likewise, following those words, he could even find a solution…

nœud nœud nœud nœud nœud nœud nœud nœud
nœud nœud nœud nœud nœud nœud
nœud nœud nœud nœud nœud nœud nœud
nœud nœud nœud nœud nœud nœud nœud nœud
nœud nœud nœud nœud nœud nœud nœud nœud nœud
nœud nœud nœud nœud nœud nœud nœud nœud nœud nœud
nœud nœud nœud nœud nœud nœud nœud nœud nœud nœud
nœud nœud nœud nœud nœud nœud nœud nœud nœud nœud
nœud nœud nœud nœud nœud nœud nœud nœud nœud nœud
nœud nœud nœud nœud nœud nœud nœud nœud nœud
nœud nœud nœud nœud nœud nœud nœud nœud nœud
nœud nœud nœud nœud nœud nœud nœud nœud nœud
nœud nœud nœud nœud nœud nœud nœud nœud nœud nœud
nœud nœud nœud nœud nœud nœud nœud nœud nœud
nœud nœud nœud nœud nœud nœud nœud nœud
nœud nœud nœud nœud nœud nœud nœud nœud
nœud nœud nœud nœud nœud nœud nœud nœud nœud

- How do I find more words written with that letter? Which are those words? - *Mœris* asked his father.

- The first thing that you should do is to consult a good dictionary, go to the city library - his father answered.

Mœris went to the city library and in a big dictionary, guiding himself by the order of the alphabet, after the "o", found those words that begin with the ligature *œ*: ecumenical *œcuménique*, edema *œdème*, eye *œil*, ox eye *œil-of-bœuf*, look *œillade*, carnation *œillet*, enology *œnologie*, enológic *œnologique*, enologist *œnologue*, esophagus *œsophage*, estrogen *œstrogène*, egg *œuf*, work *œuvre*, to work *œuvrer* and its derived; but how to find more words?..., already in his house, asking his father…

- Dad, how can I find more words that have this letter?

œil de bœuf œil de bœuf œil de bœuf œil de bœuf
œil de bœuf œil de bœuf œil de bœuf œil de bœuf
œil de bœuf œil de bœuf œil de bœuf œil de bœuf
œil de bœuf œil de bœuf œil de bœuf œil de bœuf
œil de bœuf œil de bœuf œil de bœuf œil de bœuf
œil de bœuf œil de bœuf œil de bœuf œil de bœuf
œil de bœuf œil de bœuf œil de bœuf œil de bœuf
œil de bœuf œil de bœuf œil de bœuf œil de bœuf
œil de bœuf œil de bœuf œil de bœuf œil de bœuf
œil de bœuf œil de bœuf œil de bœuf œil de bœuf
œil de bœuf œil de bœuf œil de bœuf œil de bœuf
œil de bœuf œil de bœuf œil de bœuf œil de bœuf
œil de bœuf œil de bœuf œil de bœuf œil de bœuf
œil de bœuf œil de bœuf œil de bœuf œil de bœuf
œil de bœuf œil de bœuf œil de bœuf œil de bœuf
œil de bœuf œil de bœuf œil de bœuf œil de bœuf

- I don't know; only continue looking and perhaps the words come to you. When one has a great interest in something, the information comes to you - the father who was reading the newspaper in that moment answered -. Look, also you can go to see this art exhibition titled: "Hearts and carnations" *Cœurs et œillets*, perhaps you find more of those words when seeing the works of art *œuvres d'art*, here it says that this artist includes in his works *œuvres* words written with the ligature *œ*…

Both looked at themselves for an instant, smiling, *Mœris* told his father:

- Works! *Œuvres!* That word is also written with the ligature *œ*.
Now, *Mœris* was very attentive and he was going to that art exhibition. He would look for more words, impelled by the desire *vœu* of finding the name of the illness that his mother suffered; as well as, some solution or remedy for her. He was motivated and impelled, carrying out an incessant search…

cœurs et œillets   cœurs et œillets   cœurs et œillets
cœurs et œillets   cœurs et œillets   cœurs et œillets
cœurs et œillets   cœurs et œillets   cœurs et œillets
cœurs et œillets   cœurs et œillets   cœurs et œillets
cœurs et œillets   cœurs et œillets   cœurs et œillets
cœurs et œillets   cœurs et œillets   cœurs et œillets
cœurs et œillets   cœurs et œillets   cœurs et œillets
cœurs et œillets   cœurs et œillets   cœurs et œillets

CŒURS

cœurs et œillets   cœurs et œillets   cœurs et œillets
cœurs et œillets   cœurs et œillets   cœurs et œillets
cœurs et œillets   cœurs et œillets   cœurs et œillets
cœurs et œillets   cœurs et œillets   cœurs et œillets
cœurs et œillets   cœurs et œillets   cœurs et œillets
cœurs et œillets   cœurs et œillets   cœurs et œillets
cœurs et œillets   cœurs et œillets   cœurs et œillets

Alchimie Ligature, Alchemy Ligature. It was this way how that artist's general work *œuvre* was known and "Hearts and carnations" *"Cœurs et œillets"*, the name of that particular exhibition. It was exactly, the day of the inauguration, many works of art *œuvres d'art* and people everywhere. Drawings, paintings, pictures, digital art... That artist drew and painted on paper sheets where were printed many words written with the ligature *œ*. In this occasion, the names of many flowers, scientific names in French and/or Latin. And in some works of art *œuvres d'art*, some effect deceiving *trompe-l'œil* was presented, with the digitalized images.

Mœris didn't understand anything, they were many strange words and on them: lines and stains of colors. He was devoted to also write, those names of plants on his notebook: *phœnix, pœcile, œnanthe, œnothère*. And flowers: ox eyes *œils de bœufs*, carnations *œillets*, sprouts *œilletons* and many more...

œuvres d'art œuvres d'art œuvres d'art œuvres d'art
cœurs et œillets cœurs et œillets cœurs et œillets
œuvres d'art œuvres d'art œuvres d'art œuvres d'art
cœurs et œillets cœurs et œillets cœurs et œillets
œuvres d'art œuvres d'art œuvres d'art œuvres d'art
cœurs et œillets cœurs et œillets cœurs et œillets
œuvres d'art œuvres d'art œuvres d'art œuvres d'art
cœurs et œillets cœurs et œillets cœurs et œillets
œuvres d'art œuvres d'art œuvres d'art œuvres d'art
cœurs et œillets cœurs et œillets cœurs et œillets
œuvres d'art œuvres d'art œuvres d'art œuvres d'art
cœurs et œillets cœurs e

Œ

illets cœurs et œillets
cœurs et œillets cœurs et œillets cœurs et œillets
œuvres d'art œuvres d'art œuvres d'art œuvres d'art
cœurs et œillets cœurs et œillets cœurs et œillets
œuvres d'art œuvres d'art œuvres d'art œuvres d'art
cœurs et œillets cœurs et œillets cœurs et œillets
œuvres d'art œuvres d'art œuvres d'art œuvres d'art
cœurs et œillets cœurs et œillets cœurs et œillets
œuvres d'art œuvres d'art œuvres d'art œuvres d'art
cœurs et œillets cœurs et œillets cœurs et œillets
œuvres d'art œuvres d'art œuvres d'art œuvres d'art
cœurs et œillets cœurs et œillets cœurs et œillets
œuvres d'art œuvres d'art œuvres d'art œuvres d'art

There the artist was, speaking about his work *œuvre*, while the appetizers *hors-d'œuvres* were distributed. *Mœris* ate some candies called ox eyes *œils de bœufs* exquisite, although, something luscious *écœurant* and it was distributed among the companies a Champagne of *Œuilly*.

Mœris found new words in each work of art *œuvre d'art*, he wrote them down on his notebook. After writing all those names of flowers and aquatic plants, he went to listen the artist speak about his work of art *chef-d'œuvre*. This artist explained that his main interest was a spatial problem, the fact that "two" share one same space.

-…This way, those words that are written with the ligature *œ* interested me, because, it seems that the "o" and the "e" share, or disputed the same space, they fuse and at the end, a new identity is created: the ligature *œ*. I relate the words with the images in my works *œuvres* and play with them; it is a work *œuvre* in which the text is present according to the images that I work with. Text and image fuse, creating the work *œuvre*… - the artist said, but *Mœris* wanted to know names of illnesses or remedies and he asked the artist…

ŒŒŒ ŒŒŒ

ŒŒŒ ŒŒŒ

ŒŒŒ ŒŒŒ

ŒŒŒ ŒŒŒ

ŒŒŒ ŒŒŒ

œuvres d'art œuvres d'art œuvres d'art œuvres d'art

- Do some illnesses that are written with that letter exist, Mr.? - *Mœris* asked.

- Illnesses? Yes…, there are some illnesses, as the edemas *œdèmes*; but if you want to know which are all the illnesses that are written with the ligature *œ*, it is simple, you only have to consult in the: Illustrated Dictionary of the ligature *œ* (*Dictionnaire illustré de la ligature œ*) - the artist answered.

- There is an illustrated dictionary, dedicated to the ligature *œ?!* Are all the words that are written with that letter there? - *Mœris* asked astonished.

- Yes, look... In the general dictionaries you only find some words, the most common, those that are used with frequency. In specialized books as those of medicine, you will find the medical terms that are written with the ligature *œ*; in those of agriculture equally, you will only find the terms that refer in particular to that area, some many more words; but in the illustrated Dictionary of the ligature *œ*, (*Dictionnaire illustré de la ligature œ*), you will find all the words

ŒŒŒŒŒŒ
ligature œ ligature œ ligature œ ligature œ

ligature œ ligature œ ligature œ ligature œ
ligature œ ligature œ ligature œ ligature œ
ŒŒŒŒŒŒ
ligature œ ligature œ ligature œ ligature œ

ligature œ ligature œ ligature œ ligature œ
ligature œ ligature œ ligature œ ligature œ
ŒŒŒŒŒŒ
ligature œ ligature œ ligature œ ligature œ

ligature œ ligature œ ligature œ ligature œ
ligature œ ligature œ ligature œ ligature œ
ŒŒŒŒŒŒ
ligature œ ligature œ ligature œ ligature œ

ligature œ ligature œ ligature œ ligature œ
ŒŒŒŒŒŒ
ligature œ ligature œ ligature œ ligature œ

that are written with the ligature œ, images and besides all the areas of the knowledge - the artist explained to him.

- And where do I find that dictionary? - *Mœris* asked.
- Look, I have to go; but sure you will find it in the libraries, in some bookstores, or look in Internet: illustrated virtual Dictionary of the ligature œ (*Dictionnaire virtuelle illustré de la ligature œ*) - the artist answered already retiring…

The next day *Mœris* went to the city library and there was the illustrated Dictionary of the ligature œ (*Dictionnaire illustré de la ligature œ*). He read a lot and wrote down on his notebook all the names of the illnesses that he found and went quickly to the clinic to take them to the doctors.

- Doctor! Doctor! I have thought that the illness that my mother has could be here - *Mœris* said, showing his notebook to the doctor.

- Let's see… - the doctor answered, a little thwarted and unwillingly *à contrecœur*.
He read the list of words, giving a quick glance *coup d'œil*. Soon, with face of astonishment recognized the illness,

un coup d'œil un coup d'œil un coup d'œil
un coup d'œil un coup d'œil un coup d'œil
un coup d'œil un coup d'œil un coup d'œil
un coup d'œil un coup d'œil un coup d'œil
un coup d'œil un coup d'œil un coup d'œil
un coup d'œil un coup d'œil un coup d'œil
un coup d'œil un coup d'œil un coup d'œil
un coup d'œil un coup d'œil un coup d'œil
un coup d'œil un coup d'œil un coup d'œil
un coup d'œil un coup d'œil un coup d'œil
un coup d'œil un coup d'œil un coup d'œil
un coup d'œil un coup d'œil un coup d'œil
un coup d'œil un coup d'œil un coup d'œil
un coup d'œil un coup d'œil un coup d'œil
un coup d'œil un coup d'œil un coup d'œil
un coup d'œil un coup d'œil un coup d'œil

Œ Œ Œ Œ

because he already knew about some of the symptoms that *Mœris'* mother suffered. And he left quickly…

- I should leave, thank you for your help - the doctor said, agreeing with the head and making him an approbatory blink *clin d'œil.*

Days later, in the clinic, the doctors communicated to *Mœris'* father   that his wife had an illness called: celiac *cœliaque*, besides the inadequacy of the heart *cœur* and that soon she would recover…

- Everything has been an intestinal illness, of difficult diagnostic that has caused her so many problems. A biopsy was carried out in the thin intestine and she was diagnosed with the illness: celiac *cœliaque*. Now, she must take some medications: vitamins and minerals. We will give her a coenzyme *cœnzyme* Q10, after the pregnancy, to strengthen her heart *cœur*. She will have to change her habits *mœurs* and nutritious customs. Given that she will recover soon - the doctor said.

cœliaque cœliaque cœliaque cœliaque cœliaque
cœur cœur cœur cœur cœur cœur cœur
cœliaque cœliaque cœliaque cœliaque cœliaque
cœur cœur cœur cœur cœur cœur cœur
cœliaque cœliaque cœliaque cœliaque cœliaque
cœur cœur cœur cœur cœur cœur cœur
cœliaque cœliaque cœliaque cœliaque cœliaque
cœur cœur cœur cœur cœur cœur cœur
cœliaque cœliaque cœliaque cœliaque cœliaque
cœur cœur cœur cœur cœur cœur cœur
cœliaque cœliaque cœliaque cœliaque cœliaque
cœur cœur cœur cœur cœur cœur cœur
cœliaque cœliaque cœliaque cœliaque cœliaque
cœur cœur cœur cœur cœur cœur cœur
cœliaque cœliaque cœliaque cœliaque cœliaque
cœur cœur cœur cœur cœur cœur cœur
cœliaque cœliaque cœliaque cœliaque cœliaque
cœur cœur cœur cœur cœur cœur cœur
cœliaque cœliaque cœliaque cœliaque cœliaque
cœur cœur cœur cœur cœur cœur cœur
cœliaque cœliaque cœliaque cœliaque cœliaque
cœur cœur cœur cœur cœur cœur cœur
cœliaque cœliaque cœliaque cœliaque cœliaque
cœur cœur cœur cœur cœur cœur cœur
cœliaque cœliaque cœliaque cœliaque cœliaque
cœur cœur cœur cœur cœur cœur cœur
cœliaque cœliaque cœliaque cœliaque cœliaque
cœur cœur cœur cœur cœur cœur cœur
cœliaque cœliaque cœliaque cœliaque cœliaque

Mœris who accompanied his father, saw his notebook the same one that had shown to the doctor and he realized that there the name of the illness was: Celiac *Cœliaque*, and that the solution was to give her a coenzyme *cœnzyme* Q10, among other things, to change her habits *mœurs* and nutritious customs... The illness and the solution were - like *Mœris* foresaw - words that were written with the ligature *œ*.

Nine months later... *Mœris'* mother was a lot better and his little sister *sœurette* had already been born, who was dressed in a very attractive way *Tape-à-l'œil,* she shone a group with several eyelets *œillets* in shape of a heart *cœur. Mœris!* - His parents said - did you Already choose the name for your little sister *sœurette?* - Yes! - *Mœris* answered, taking out his notebook in a blink of the eyes *clin d'œil,* and tossing it a quick look *un coup d'œil -*

sœurette sœurette sœurette sœurette sœurette
clœlia clœlia clœlia clœlia clœlia clœlia
clœlia clœlia clœlia clœlia clœlia clœlia
clœlia clœlia clœlia clœlia clœlia clœlia
clœlia clœlia clœlia clœlia clœlia clœlia
clœlia clœlia clœlia clœlia clœlia clœlia
clœlia clœlia clœlia clœlia clœlia clœlia

Clœlia

clœlia clœlia clœlia clœlia clœlia clœlia
clœlia clœlia clœlia clœlia clœlia clœlia
clœlia clœlia clœlia clœlia clœlia clœlia
clœlia clœlia clœlia clœlia clœlia clœlia
clœlia clœlia clœlia clœlia clœlia clœlia
clœlia clœlia clœlia clœlia clœlia clœlia
clœlia clœlia clœlia clœlia clœlia clœlia
clœlia clœlia clœlia clœlia clœlia clœlia
sœurette sœurette sœurette sœurette sœurette

- I found it in a very special dictionary: the illustrated Dictionary of the ligature æ (*Dictionnaire illustré de la ligature æ*). Dad, Mom… How do you like the name: *Clælia?* Like this a Roman virgin of the antiquity was named…

- *Clælia!* - His parents said, giving themselves a blink *clin d'œil,* and approving the decision of *Mæris…*

Mæris had learned to trust himself, to listen to his heart *cœur* and to work *œuvrer*, without any type of rancor *rancœur*.

The end

Text and illustrations: Jorge A. Rodríguez (JAR)
First Edition 2007 Second Edition 2015
All rights reserved, Copyright © 2015 Jorge A. Rodríguez (JAR)
Translation: Froila Gómez
ISBN-13: 978-1511556668
ISBN-10: 1511556668
E-mail: jarrodriguezve@gmail.com
Facebook: Jorge A. Rodriguez Jar
Twitter: @jar_rodriguez

OTHER WORKS AUTHOR

MŒRIS AND ILLUSTRATED DICTIONARY OF LIGATURE Œ

MŒRIS AT THE MUSEUM OF THE LIGATURE Œ

MŒRIS AND THE SECRET OF DOLLAR LIGATURE Œ

www.ingramcontent.com/pod-product-compliance
Lightning Source LLC
Chambersburg PA
CBHW040748200526
45159CB00023B/1772